FRANK
NEWBOULD

RUTH ARTMONSKY

COMMERCIAL ART

**THE JOURNAL THAT CHARTED
20TH CENTURY BRITISH DESIGN**

Commercial Art
The Journal that Charted 20th Century British Design

Published by Artmonsky Arts
Flat 1, 27 Henrietta Street
London WC2E 8NA
Telephone: +44 (0)7767 820406
Email: artmonskyruth@gmail.com

www.ruthartmonsky.com

The Jacket of this book is based on the cover
design of *Commercial Art*, October 1930

The illustration opposite the title page is
a detail of the Frank Newbould cover design
for *Commercial Art*, March 1925

The illustration opposite the foreword
is a detail of the Anna Zinkeisen cover
design, August 1925

ISBN 978-1-9163845-7-6

Designed by Webb & Webb Design Limited
www.webbandwebb.co.uk

Printed in Great Britain

CONTENTS

FOREWORD

What seems eons ago, long before lockdown and before the restricted mobility of old age, on a Sunday morning each month, I would visit the National Hotel in Bloomsbury.

There, I, an oldish woman, would patiently stand in a queue with a lot of oldish men, (rarely a woman in sight), waiting for the salon doors to open at ten; all of us eager, ready to sprint if necessary, or as well as we might. For what? – for second-hand books; to see what the latest finds were, and to get to them first. Quite a grotesque scene you might think, worthy of a Goya.

I, having entered, would saunter nonchalantly along the aisles, apparently indifferent to the frenzy going on around me. After about half an hour I would drop, exhausted, on to one of two chairs by the stall of the redoubtable Chris Mees – he always had two chairs – one for himself and one for his potential customer.

Chris was THE dealer specializing in graphic design and illustrated books. An ex-university librarian he was spending his retirement putting relevant journals on line and setting up a system of access by subscription.

Chris would spring up on my arrival, for he knew a sucker when he saw one. With enthusiasm he would thrust his latest finds under my nose, turning pages to show me the treasures within. Although being a dealer he would hope to make a profit, he would genuinely want to share his enjoyment and his knowledge; even when I refused to buy.

On one such morning, Chris put into my hands a bound volume of magazines, the cover blue, with the title in gold – *Commercial Art*. I, being a novice, sat and thumbed through it, delighting in the illustrations and wondering at the mix of subjects included. Chris then informed me that he had forty such volumes covering the years 1926 to 1959, and that they were going for a song (it turned out more like an opera)!

Now I have only to know that there is a set or series of something to immediately become interested; my bookcases, at the time, were full of 19th and 20th century sets of novels. It was not long before these were cleared to accommodate my new purchase, variously named, over the years, *Commercial Art*, *Commercial Art & Industry*, *Art & Industry* and *Design for Industry*. And it was not very long afterwards that Chris, ever generous, put me in touch with another dealer, and I was actually able to buy bound volumes, this time in red, of the original *Commercial Art* before The Studio Ltd. became its owner.

As my nearest and dearest would be pouring over *Vogue* and *House and Garden*, these bound journals became a major source of pleasure for me in relaxed moments; and, when I began to write on design, a major source of information and inspiration.

Now, to own even one issue of *Commercial Art*, let alone over thirty years of them, would take anything but a modest sum. As Chris shared his pleasure in them with me, I am here attempting to share mine with the reader. Not only are they a delight in themselves, but they chart what was happening in many areas of design, both nationally, and, to some extent, internationally, in the first half of the 20th century.

Above Small format wartime and post-war paper rationing editions
Covers by Abram Games, Eric Fraser, F.H.K.Henrion, and Tom Eckersley
Opposite *Commercial Art* 1920s covers designed by G.Barraclough, Aubrey Hammond, Tom Purvis, Fraser, Austin Cooper, Ludwig Hohlwein

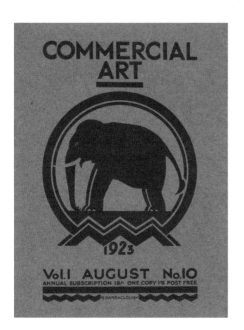

COMMERCIAL ART

1923

Vol.1 AUGUST No.10
ANNUAL SUBSCRIPTION 18/- ONE COPY 1/6 POST FREE

COMMER-CIAL ART

AUBREY HAMMOND

SEPTEMBER 1924 1/- NEW SERIES No 5

BLOCKS BY W.G.BRIGGS & Co. W.C2

COMMERCIAL ART

ORDERS ORDERS ORDERS

TOM PURVIS

OCTOBER 1924 VOLUME 3 NUMBER 6 PRICE 7D

BLOCKS BY W.G.BRIGGS & CO W.C2

COMMERCIAL ART

VOL 4 NUMBER SIX APRIL 15TH 1925 7D

BLOCKS BY W.G.BRIGGS & CO. LTD. W.C.2

COMMERCIAL ART

PRINTING EXHIBITION NUMBER
MAY 1925 1'6D

PRINTED ON MARINONI-VOIRIN OFFSET

'COMMERCIAL ART PRINTING PUBLICITY

1926

VOL 5 NO 3 9d FEBRY. 1926
BLOCKS BY W.G.BRIGGS & CO.LTD. W.C.2

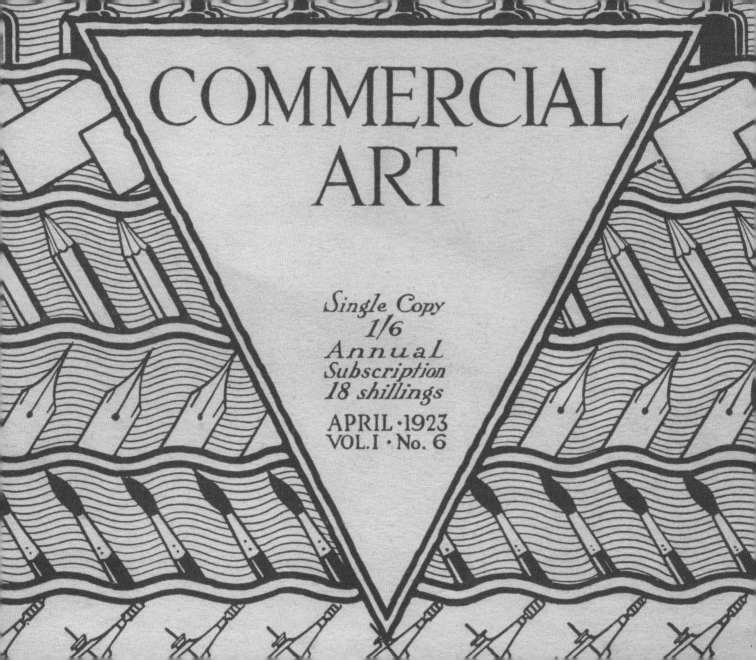

THE ORIGINAL
COMMERCIAL ART

➡ ➡ ➡ ➡ ➡ ➡ ➡ ➡ ➡

T he first issue of the journal *Commercial Art* arrived in October 1922, published from 37 Drury Lane, the offices of a company calling itself *Commercial Art Ltd.* Little is known either about the company or the exact circumstances of the journal's conception, but from the very first issue the reader is made aware of its purpose – its ambition being to marry art and commerce to the benefit of all concerned. The Editor starts his copy throwing down the gauntlet–

> *'There are some fastidious people who will not suffer the term 'Commercial Art' being used in their presence. They contend that the two words antagonize one another and cannot be joined without some sort of sacrilege being committed.'*

Opposite Cover designed by Bernard J. Palmer

COMMERCIAL ART

A MAGAZINE DEVOTED TO ART AS A SELLING FORCE

A masterly booklet cover design by Herrick, of The Baynard Press, for the R.M.S.P.

CONTENTS

JUNE, 1924 · VOL. III · New Series No. 2

ALL COMMUNICATIONS with reference to COMMERCIAL ART
whether in connection with editorial, advertising, circulation, or general business matters should be
addressed to 37 DRURY LANE, LONDON, W.C.2. *Telephone:* Regent 5251

29

Contents page incorporating poster illustration by Herrick

By the third issue he is in full flood –

'Art is RIGHT, that it makes for trade, for reputation, that it establishes good will or that it is the means by which a business or a State can manifest its superiority then shall we not be justified in investing in Art, not as a matter of enthusiasm alone, but for reasons of real expediency.'

After a year's publication, in the October 1923 journal, a definite smugness enters the editorial –

'We have just completed our first year and like a healthy young baby that everyone cherishes and admires we have made a large number of friends. From them we learn that we have accomplished a great many things it was our object to attain.'

He then proceeds to list some of these – the improved 'get ups' of British and foreign press advertisements, more attractive hoardings, the press covering subjects first raised in the journal, and more of the same. He even suggests that Americans, coming over for a forthcoming advertising convention to be held in London, might well be impressed by the way standards had been raised, implying, by the efforts of the journal –

'that we have got something to show which we can do as well as they themselves can do it –nearly.'

Before and after retouched photo – photography
as a technique rather than an art

use of colour and of photography, were made much of, the latter simply explained technically and argued for practical advantages, rather than, as later, treated as artistry.

And graphics would also be covered with features on products – posters, press advertisements, booklets (sales and publicity brochures), packaging, folders, calendars, and so on. Much space was given to a curiosity of the time, the poster stamp, a perforated stamp, illustrated as a poster might be, but in miniature, that could be stuck anywhere, onto envelopes, correspondence, invoices, and such, as an additional form of advertising.

And the editor appreciated that if commercial art was to become a profession, graphic designers would need to

The reader was not only made aware of the crusading tone likely to imbue further issues, but the content to be covered. The journal was not going to concern itself with all aspects of design, but would focus on graphics (then known as 'commercial art'); and declared that it would 'deal comprehensively with all branches of it'. And, during its lifetime it largely kept to this, approaching the subject from as many angles as possible – articles on the actual production of work, such matters as layout, typography, and to a lesser extent illustration, were always included, along with methods of reproduction. Two relatively new aspects at that time – the

Poster stamps, 1920s

BITS FROM EVERYWHERE

The first regular news feature, 1923

understand the management of their operations, so a number of organizational issues were raised, as copyright of work, the role of a design director, relationships with commissioners and printers, and the training of new entrants. On this latter the Editor seems to have taken a pragmatic view –

'Genius will always free itself from the fetters of an organized system of study and go one better than the rank and file; but the business man who lacks experience and judgement will be able to put his trust in the certified artist and designer and save himself disappointment.'

It would be some time before such a nationally recognized 'certification' came into being and came to be accepted.

Commercial Art soon settled to a standard format – the rabble rousing, but short, editorial, to be followed by well-

CANDID
COMMENTS

By Loraine Conran

1930s feature, George Loraine Conran became the director of Manchester City Art Galleries in 1962

illustrated articles and examples of good practice, along with advertisements from all and sundry – artists' agents, art book publishers, printers, advertising agencies – it even had columns for 'small' advertisements such as 'young lady, experienced, seeks commissions as Poster and Showcard designer'; or 'Ex-chief copywriter to Leading Agency writes Pamphlets, Sales Letters for Advertisers; remarkable results'.

There were always miscellaneous news items that didn't quite fit in with the body of the copy and, over the years, were massed under a number of cute titles, the first being 'Bits from Everywhere'. Such snippets might include a criticism of a recent poster, or an item about an art school, down to such gossip as a golf ball crashing through the artist Gregory Brown's studio skylight. In the 1930s Loraine Conran became the regular writer for this section, initially titled 'Candid Comments, things that please and things that annoy', later to be shortened to just 'Commentary'.

In its first issue the Editor states his position on the criterion for including articles –

'…select MSS and drawings for this publication solely on their merit, whether the writers are well known in Commercial Art Circles or have yet to make their name.'

But articles, it seems, did not come flooding in, and the magazine started to approach advertisers, such as Pear's Soap, Libby's Milk, Johnny Walker, Shell and HMV, to demonstrate that being featured in *Commercial Art* could be

Shell illustration by Edmund J. Sullivan, 1923, to attract other companies to contribute to the magazine

❖ ARTISTS WHO HELP THE ADVERTISER ❖

considered virtually free advertising. Eventually the Editor felt it necessary to make a direct appeal –

'…we ask our friends to appreciate our own efforts… and to collaborate with us in the propagation of our magazine. We want them to supply us with suitable editorial and artistic material and to fill our advertising pages with announcements expressing their artistic aspirations while stating the particulars of their service.'

And it would seem that the response was satisfactory, for soon potential features were pouring in from all quarters – from advertising agencies, printers, manufacturers and retailers, and occasionally from artists themselves.

Some contributors came to be regular feature writers as G.M.Ellwood (a furniture designer as well as a commercial artist) on retail display, and Adolphe Arnaud Brown on the contribution of individual artists to advertising work. So familiar did Mr. Brown become that either he, or the editor, decided it was sufficient to merely use the initials A.A.B. for readers to immediately recognize the author. A few contributors appeared so frequently as Eric N. Simmons and R.J.Kelly, writing on a range of subjects, that it is possible that some were not freelance but in the employment of Commercial Art Ltd itself; but that is only surmise.

With hindsight several of the early contributors to *Commercial Art* had, or came to have, significance in the commercial art world. R.P.Gossop was here, there, and everywhere at the time – commercial artist himself, running an artists' agency (Eric Fraser in his stable), with a track record as studio manager with W.H.Smith, the first art editor of the British *Vogue* and a founder member of the Society of Industrial Artists. He was to write a book specifically on advertisement design, in 1927.

And then there were the redoubtable William Gamble and R.B.Fishenden, both with printing backgrounds, each to be longstanding editors of *Penrose Annual*, Gamble its original editor and Fishenden steering it for some twenty years (from 1934 to 1957) towards its becoming as much a vehicle for graphic design as for printing. A later freelance contributor to *Commercial Art* was the South African born G.H.Saxon Mills, 'Bingy' to his friends and colleagues. Saxon Mills brought a journalists' view to the magazine, but a journalist with an aesthetic streak. When, in 1924, he joined the Crawford

Opposite Feature and illustration by G.M.Ellwood

THE SELLING WINDOW

PART THREE—HATS
by G. M. Ellwood, S.G.A.

FIG. 7.

advertising agency as copywriter, he was to tie in with Ashley Havinden and Margaret Sangster (later Mrs. Havinden) to form a tightly bound trio, writer, artist and account executive, one of the most successful advertising teams in the inter-war years; it was Saxon Mills who was to write a biography of the great man himself, Sir William Crawford.

Although *Commercial Art* set out to get business people to make use of artists and artists to change their attitudes to working commercially, by featuring examples, the magazine accidentally, or perhaps intentionally, was helping artists build their reputations by such exposure. In the second series, from 1923, the feature 'Artists Who Help The Advertiser' began to appear, and, in fact, continued to appear in most of the issues to come. The list of artists so selected now reads like a roll call of the most illustrious British commercial artists of the first half of the 20th century – some, at the time, already fairly well-established, some just breaking in, a mere handful now completely forgotten. Some, such as Edmund J. Sullivan and Aldo Cosmati, fairly traditional in style, others such as Gregory Brown, Tom Purvis and Austin Cooper moving towards modernism, and then, McKnight Kauffer, the leader of the pack, when it came to avant garde. And the magazine was perhaps prescient in featuring four of the five artists to gain exclusive contracts with LNER, a novel arrangement for commercial artists at the time – Austin Cooper, Frank Newbould, Tom Purvis and Fred Tayor, only Frank Mason missed by the astute editor.

Few women featured in the original *Commercial Art* – Dora Batty perhaps more of an illustrator, Mrs Barraclough

Label design by Mrs G. Barraclough for a Manchester textile company, illustrating an article 'Animals in Advertising', 1923

VIM

MIGHTY ATOMS OF DIRTSHIFTING
ENERGY—THAT'S VIM ★ VIM CLEANS
POTS ⋅ PANS ⋅ CUTLERY ⋅ CROCKERY
BATHS AND SINKS ⋅ TILES AND
PORCELAIN ⋅ GLAZED AND EN-
AMELLED SURFACES ⋅ FLOORS AND
TABLES ⋅ DISHES ⋅ COOKING VESSELS
COOKING STOVES AND ALL KITCHEN
UTENSILS : MAKES THEM LIKE NEW
★ ★ VIM WHIZZES DIRT AWAY ★ ★
LEVER BROTHERS LIMITED
PORT SUNLIGHT

The editor's favoured designer McKnight Kauffer – a controversial
advertisement for VIM scouring powder, 1925

already providing posters for London Transport in the early 1920s as well as carrying out other commercial work, and the Zinkeisen sisters – described as 'two clever sisters whose work will live as long as advertising itself'. Anna gets most of the attention with her work for Schweppes, Wedgwood and London Transport; Doris really only mentioned for her work with the theatre. Both were later to hit the headlines with their decorative work for shipping lines, including providing murals for the Queen Mary.

The magazine also acted as a kind of newspaper, recording events, commenting on them in advance, at the time, and on reflection afterwards. The editor would grasp at anything going on that could be seen to have some relevance to commercial art. Whatever the relatively short-lived government British Institute of Industrial Art was doing (BIIA only recently established in 1920 to encourage better design) was noted in a slightly patronising tone, as when it put on an exhibition –

'We should like to take this opportunity of congratulating the British Institute of Industrial Art on its work of genuine national service...'

The editor focused, in his comments, on the graphic arts section of the exhibition, particularly mentioning the major presses of the day – Baynard, Cloister, Curwen, Morland, and Pelican. And when it came to graphic artists the editor put McKnight Kauffer's work, on show there, well above the rest. To ensure that *Commercial Art* was linked in the reader's mind

to what was going on at government level, he declared that BIIA had –

> 'the very same ideal for which we are striving and shall go on striving.'

Yet again, in 1924, the editor lines up his magazine with government activity, this time with the gigantic British Empire Exhibition to be held at Wembley, declaring it a triumph as far as commercial art was concerned. His editorial in May suggests that the Wembley site had been visited a number of times by the magazine's staff, and uses italics to stress the importance of the exhibition to the magazine's raison d'etre –

> 'Commercial Art *takes a very serious interest in the British Empire Exhibition, because it is the first important Exhibition in this country in which the need for artistic arrangement has been fully recognized.*'

So key was the exhibition to *Commercial Art* that it was decided to devote –

> 'a special number of this magazine, dealing with the exhibits which are most interesting from the aesthetic point of view.'

Opposite Drawing of British Empire Exhibition site by Sydney R. Jones

British Empire Exhibition number, cover design by Austin Cooper, 1924

COMMERCIAL ART IN ENGLAND AND AMERICA

A DIFFERENCE IN ATTITUDE

by Brian Rowe, Partner in Langham Artists

A typical example of the American style of poster. It is drawn with the utmost care and realism, and is printed equally carefully, regardless of cost of production.

American poster design, 1924

Herrick's lion – the symbol of the British Empire exhibition

The issue for June 1924 did just that. The Editor did not hold back on declaring that grand as the Exhibition was, the advertising for it was weak –

'It lacks the vision, it lacks the spirit of enthusiasm, the sweeping gesture that embraces the skies and the universe. It is tame and humdrum.'

Commercial Art was also to devote a good deal of space to the International Advertising Convention that was being held in London at the same time. It had already previously featured and supported Sir Charles Higham's plea that London should be the chosen venue –

'He wanted to see Great Britain receive those delegates wholeheartedly, and every man and woman in advertising play a part in it so that the whole Convention would be a credit to Great Britain.'

– very much singing from the same song sheet that the magazine was using. The Editor strongly endorsed Higham's proposal, this time lining his journal up with one of the key figures in the advertising industry.

With the Convention taking place in London, it was decided that the magazine issues for August and September should largely be devoted to it and to the accompanying Exhibition of Advertising Art, with its Poster Street, which was mounted at the Wembley site, the editor alerting his readers –

COMMERCIAL ART

VOL 4 No-10   PRICE 9d NET   AUGUST 1925

BLOCKS BY W.G.BRIGGS & CO. LTD. W.C.2

Above Anna Zinkeisen cover, 1925

Opposite A loose insert advertising publisher, paper company and printer.

Designed by Edward Bawden for William Heinemann, 1925

'Our representatives will attend these conferences and summarise them for the benefit of our readers in the next issue.'

– which it proceeded to do, along with comments on the Palace of the Arts exhibition, which was panned for its 'lack of ideas', whilst Poster Street was only considered 'good in parts'.

Americans travelling over for the Convention led to comments on what was going on beyond our shores in commercial art. The magazine had generally focused its energies and enthusiasms on the British scene, with just the odd snippet on European examples from time to time; but from the Convention onwards, included American. None of this would compare with the strong internationalism of the magazine when it came under new ownership.

Why *Commercial Art* was sold to The Studio Ltd. is not clear. Perhaps, set up with the aim to bring 'art' and 'commerce' together, it considered that it had gone a good way along that route – stirring the torpid manufacturer, demonstrating to the printers that they could have designing as well as technical competences, and persuading the artists that they could be making a major contribution to society by accepting briefs and yet retain outlets for their creative egos; or perhaps it was simply from financial necessity. Whichever, the last issue of the original *Commercial Art* was issued in June 1926.

Travel   Autumn List   Bio-graphy

William Heinemann LTD

Poetry   Fiction

1925

Ed. Bawden

NOVEL COVER FOR A PUBLISHER'S CATALOGUE

reproduced by the courtesy of

Messrs. Wm. Heinemann Ltd.

This is printed on
ABBEY MILLS GREENFIELD
ANTIQUE LAID
Supplied by
GROSVENOR CHATER & Co., Ltd

Printed from Two Colour Line Blocks
by
H. J. GOSS & CO., LTD.
Printers of Quality
299-301, GRAY'S INN ROAD
LONDON W.C.1

Founder, Charles Holme, and son, Geoffrey, who succeeded him at The Studio Ltd.

THE STUDIO LTD

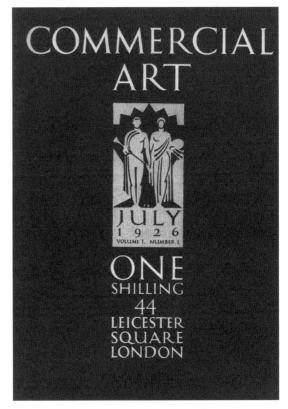

I n July 1926 the first issue of *Commercial Art* under its new ownership was published. Bryan Holme, writing of his grandfather's and father's contributions to the development of The Studio Ltd., gives no account of why, when it was still trying to revive its fortunes after WWI, the publisher would venture so far into the world of commerce and industry, straying from its relatively 'fine art' realm.

The Studio Ltd., like Commercial Art Ltd. was founded on idealism, but whereas the latter merely wanted to restore Britain's economic power through art, the founder of The Studio Ltd., Charles Holme, had worldly ambitions. Working as a merchant in the Far East he developed a passion for the *objets d'art* of the different cultures he visited. He came to see language as the barrier between nations understanding each other and felt that if countries could be made aware of other cultures visually, there would be mutual understanding and world peace!

New series, Volume 1, Number 1
published by The Studio Ltd.

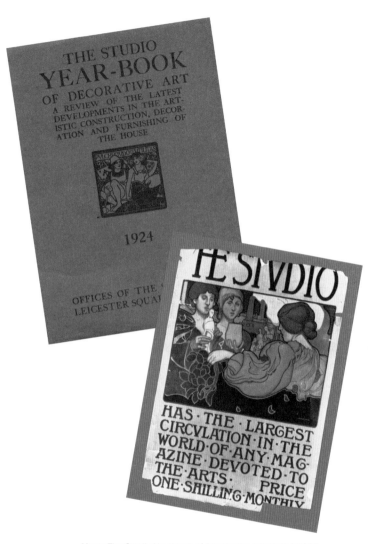

THE STUDIO
YEAR-BOOK
OF DECORATIVE ART
A REVIEW OF THE LATEST
DEVELOPMENTS IN THE ART-
ISTIC CONSTRUCTION, DECOR-
ATION AND FURNISHING OF
THE HOUSE

1924

OFFICES OF THE
LEICESTER SQUAR

HE STVDIO

HAS·THE·LARGEST
CIRCVLATION·IN·THE
WORLD·OF·ANY·MAG-
AZINE·DEVOTED·TO
THE·ARTS.
ONE·SHILLING·MONTHLY
PRICE

Above The Studio Yearbook of Decorative Art annual 1924
Below Poster for The Studio by Frank Brangwyn

Holme began to develop the idea of an art magazine to serve this end, setting up his business at 44 Leicester Square. He was lucky enough to have a business manager, Frank Alfred Mercer whose enthusiasm led him, in addition, to take on the role of editor; and equally fortunate to have a son, Geoffrey, who was to completely immerse himself in the company. The Company seems to have tested the ground in advance for The Studio Ltd. by publishing an annual, variously titled *Posters and their Designers*, *Posters and Publicity*, *Art & Publicity,* from 1924. These were astounding publications for they must had introduced many readers to examples of European and American advertising for the very first time. In fact, by the time The Studio Ltd. took over *Commercial Art* it had a considerable history in publishing journals and books on both the 'fine 'and the 'applied' arts. It had begun publishing the monthly journal *The Studio* in 1893, its book publishing started in 1894; and, in 1906, it put out the annual *The Studio Yearbook of Decorative Art*.

Whatever the motivation for purchasing an already established journal on commercial art, the immediate impact on the editing of the journal was that it went international (which after all had been the company founder's original aim), although this was barely touched upon in the first editorial –

'the object is to be of service to the business man, the designer and the general public. It will show the manufacturer, retailer and advertiser what is being accomplished at home and abroad and make them familiar with the work of artists and designers who can help them. It will place

MON SAVON...

C'EST...

"MONSAVON"

Jean Carlu poster for soap, 1928

the commercial point of view before the artist, and assist him to realize the needs of commerce and the conditions of mechanical reproduction. It will show the public that it is interested in beautiful things, products of everyday utility which they can buy produced at competitive prices, and yet possess the fine essential qualities of a work of art.'

Commercial Art Ltd. could not have put it better themselves. The 'internationalism', although not mentioned in the editorial, actually flooded the first issue, with examples from America, Austria, France, Hungary, Germany and Japan. And there were early hints that the journal's range might extend beyond graphic and display design towards the design of products – from Rolls Royce cars and locomotives to pottery and kitchen utensils. Some years before the term 'industrial design' was coined the new owners of *Commercial Art* began pleading its cause –

'…it is a sad truism that the designedly beautiful things of this world are in nine cases out of ten utterly useless or 'too good to use'; while the designedly useful things are either positively ugly or negatively plain.'

Although readers could be stirred by the new direction its old magazine was taking, they would still see familiar features on posters, press advertisements, printers, window displays, photography, Shell and Lever Bros., McKnight Kauffer and Tom Purvis; and articles by Gossop. And the concept of series was continued as with 'Aspects of the Selling Art', 'Men who

Rolls Royce 'New Phantom' and kitchen utensils for 'Art and Commerce'
article, 1926 – an early interest in industrial design

Create Advertising' and 'Celebrities in Advertising' – the last including some of the luminaries of the time – Frank Pick of the Underground, Charles Higham, Harold Vernon and William Crawford, advertising agents, Cecil Dandridge of LNER, Fred Taylor artist, and G. Russell Chairman of the Advertising Association. Artists considered worth featuring singly, in the issues in the last years of the 1920s, included Charles Paine, Tom Purvis, Spenser Pryse, Aubrey Hammond, and Horace Taylor; and, from abroad, A.M. Cassandre, Jean Carlu and Paul Colin – McKnight Kauffer towering over them all.

The printers most frequently mentioned by *Commercial Art* for the design quality of their work were The Curwen Press, The Westminster Press, The Pelican Press, along with A. Tolmer of Paris. Whilst the companies featured for their well-designed publicity and advertising included Shell (both before and after the arrival of Jack Beddington), the Royal Mail Steam Packet Company, Sundour textiles, Southern Rail, LNER, the Underground, and MacFisheries. When it came to car advertising, an ever favourite subject of *Commercial Art*, Vauxhall and Cadillac seem to have been the flavour of the period.

But then came the news of the publicity work of a maverick governmental agency, the Empire Marketing Board (EMB), recently established in 1926. Among other aims the Board had been set up to boost sales of Empire products, and although it set about this in a variety of ways – press advertising, exhibitions, shopping weeks and such like – it was the Board's posters to which *Commercial Art* was to give considerable space over the seven years of the Board's

Men Who Create Advertising

Mr. C. G. G. Dandridge

Drawing by 'bil'

Mr. Frank Pick

Drawing by 'bil'

Mr. H. Gordon Selfridge

Drawing by 'bil'

Sir William S. Crawford, K.B.E.

Drawing by 'bil'

The Right Hon. C. A. McCurdy, K.C.

Drawing by Aubrey Hammond

Mr. Fred Taylor, R.I.

Drawing by Henry Ospovat

Sir Charles F. Higham

Drawing by 'Aubrey Hammond

Mr. C. Harold Vernon

Drawing by 'Aubrey Hammond

existence. With Frank Pick chairing its poster committee along with William Crawford and the 'imaginative civil servant' Stephen Tallents, it challenged government attitudes as to the vulgarity of advertising and set a precedence for future government publicity when Tallents left to become Publicity Manager for the General Post Office.

The EMB posters were not designed to blanket sell, but more to 'mobilise a sentiment' as Crawford termed it – 'to make the Empire come alive' to people, to ready their minds for more direct selling. The EMB posters did little, if anything, to better poster design for they were largely made up of illustrations of Empire food growing and manufacturing scenes – a Canadian harvest, a South African orange grove and similar by such artists as Spenser Pryse, Gregory Brown, Fred Taylor, and McKnight Kauffer, by now familiar to readers of the magazine.

But the Board's posters, by being specially framed and hung on hoardings, were to set a standard for poster display and, more importantly, the Board demonstrated to other parts of the Government the impact good publicity could have, when up until then publicity was generally considered vulgar and not for government. With Tallents taking his enthusiasm and expertise on to the General Post Office, 'singing EMB's song in a strange land', the flood doors were open, so that by the onset of WWII nearly every government department had a publicity policy and some, even their own publicity operation.

The original *Commercial Art* had carried snippets on relevant exhibitions and fairs, but with the new ownership mere brief commentary grew to become full-blown articles. From the first The Studio Ltd issue, the magazine allotted increasing space to cover exhibitions – national and international, broadly based or focused specifically on advertising and publicity. The Board of Trade had, only relatively recently, in 1920, begun to hold its annual British Industries Fair (BIF) for two weeks every spring on sites in Castle Bromwich and London – 'showing the world the strength of British industry, the craftsmanship, design and quality'. These were essentially trade fairs, but the public was admitted between certain hours. These general fairs received regular mention in *Commercial Art*, comments covering overall exhibition design as well as the presentations of different companies and organisations and their products, but usually focusing on graphics – aspects of advertising and publicity. The Advertising Association, founded in 1924, held its own annual exhibitions at Olympia and these were also to be given full coverage in the magazine.

When it came to overseas exhibitions The Studio Ltd reported on such general ones as the Leipzig Fair, but gave full coverage to the relevantly focused Art Director's Club of New York annual shindig. This was first held in 1921 (a year after the Club itself was founded), with the aim 'to dignify the field of business art in the eye of the artist'. Over the years, it was perhaps the most regularly and fully illustrated exhibition featured in *Commercial Art*, often allotted more than half a dozen pages.

In considering exhibitions and fairs *Commercial Art* did not hold back on its comments, or curry favours. A typical

'Bananas–The British West Indies', Poster designed by McKnight Kauffer

for the Empire Marketing Board, 1926

A *Commercial Art* exhibition stand, 1927

response to a BIF show, in 1927, was, whilst commending the EMB's stand at the entrance –'This dignified scheme…put the visitor into an excellent frame of mind for investigating the rest of the exhibition' – went on to bemoan the manufactured products on show – 'the decorative interest is often disappointing, and suggests that many producers are out of touch with modern educated tastes and insufficiently aware of improved aesthetic standards' – thereby implying their own 'in touchness' and 'awareness' of such matters.

When it came to exhibition designers, the magazine brought to the notice of readers the work of a budding young architect, Joseph Emberton, who had already designed kiosks for the British Empire Exhibition, and was now becoming responsible for overall exhibition layouts and for the standardization of exhibition stands, as for the Advertising Exhibitions held at Olympia.

So expert had *Commercial Art* become in the do's and don'ts of exhibition design and display stands, that before the end of the decade the whole of an editorial page, using three different sizes of type, announced that it was not the British Government or the Design & Industries Association or the Royal Society of Arts that the Italian Government had

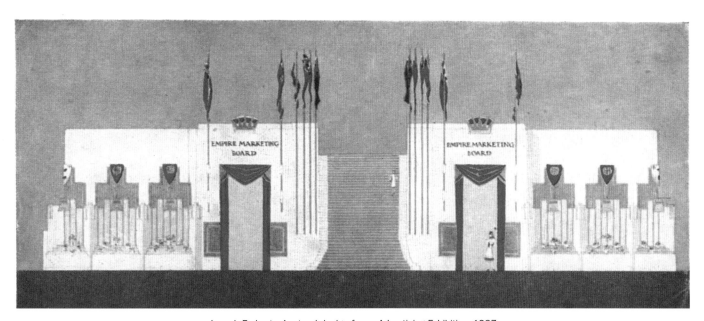

Joseph Emberton's stand design for an Advertising Exhibition, 1927

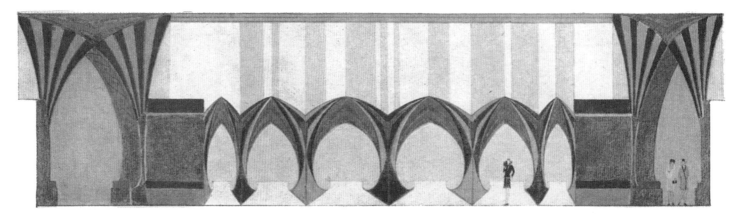

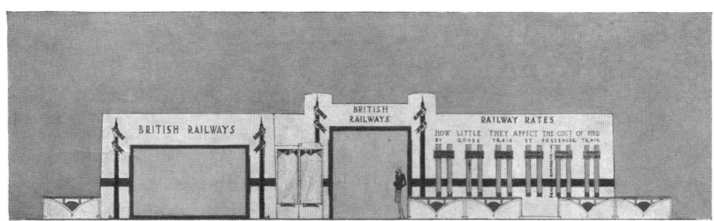

Joseph Emberton's stand designs for an Advertising Exhibition, 1927

approached to design the British section of the following year's Monza Fair, but the magazine itself! There was more than a hint of smugness in its declaring –

'The fest will not, we imagine, be other than satisfying to the British advertisers, agents, designers and printers, among whom we are proud to feel that the magazine has already established a secure place as an index of merit, a record of progress, and the disinterested friend of the best type of publicity wherever it is to be found.'

What is so amazing about the management of the magazine by The Studio Ltd. was that it virtually had the same name attached to its editorship throughout its life. F.A.Mercer, joined the company as its business manager but was soon, in addition to this, to take on the role of editor of the magazine. Beginning in the late 1920s, along with W.Gaunt as co-editor, through to the onset of WWII he ran the ship; and with the onset of war he was first to be assisted by Robert Harling, the typographer, and then by Grace Lovat Fraser, before working on his own. When the war ended, Rathbone Holme, Geoffrey's son, seems to have worked with Mercer on the editing, through to the mid 1950s. For the issues in 1956 Mercer is described as consultant editor, with Rathbone as editor, Mercer retiring in the October. For the short remainder of the magazine's life Wilfred Walter took over the reins through to the magazines rebranding as *Design for Industry* in 1959 when the editor is named as Robert

Frank Mercer, Director of The Studio Ltd. and long time editor of *Commercial Art/Art & Industry*

Downer (Walter becoming the general editor for the company) and it now having a woman art editor Margaret Webb named.

So indispensable did Mercer become to The Studio Ltd. that it was he who was dispatched to New York to set up Studio Publications Inc. its American arm. Eventually Mercer was to become Managing Director of The Studio Ltd itself. On his retirement the magazine described him as –

'responsible for shaping and enlarging the editorial policy of this publication for more than thirty years.'

Although not a designer himself, Mercer was to be voted a Fellow of the Society of Industrial Artists and, in 1959, to receive the Royal Society of Arts Bicentenary Medal which was given to non-industrial designers who, in the opinion of the RSA Council –

'exerted exceptional influence in promoting art and design in British industry.'

– an accolade to him and to the magazine.

W. Gaunt, never with his first name spelt out, is generally assumed to be the same William Gaunt, the art historian of the Pre-Raphaelites. If this were so, then he, an Oxford graduate with an academic bent, would seem to be an odd bed-fellow for Mercer – 'an astute business man' – albeit Gaunt, whose father had been a graphic designer, would have had some relevant knowledge of the demands of what publishing such a magazine as *Commercial Art* would be. Whatever the differences in personality and interest, they seemed to have worked well together for more than a decade, both editing *Commercial Art* and other The Studio Ltd. publications as *Poster Progress*, in 1939, with its introduction by Tom Purvis.

Grace Lovat Fraser, who assisted Mercer in the early 1940s is usually footnoted as merely the wife, and then the widow of Claud, but she was much more than that. An American, who had worked as a singer, actress and stage designer before her marriage, actually worked with her husband on set and costume designs, and, herself, set up a business designing for theatres, fashion and interiors. She was later to work in the Research and Industrial Design department of the advertising agency Pritchard, Wood & Partners. With artistic skills, and some four languages, she would have been a considerable help to Mercer, albeit for a relatively short time.

By the end of the 1920s the editors would have been well-pleased with their efforts. They had relaunched *Commercial Art* in a better printed, better designed, format; they had expanded its range of interests; and they had introduced its readers to the international scene. So confident had they become that they decided to give *Commercial Art* its own annual, as it were – *Modern Publicity*. Building on their previous attempts at annuals, focusing only on graphics, *Modern Publicity* maintained the internationalism of the company with sections on what was going on in the graphic arts in most European countries as well as in North and South America and beyond.

Opposite Covers for long-running *Modern Publicity* annual, published by The Studio Ltd.

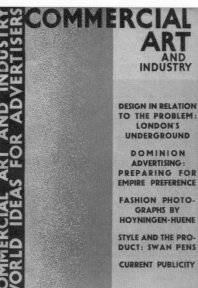

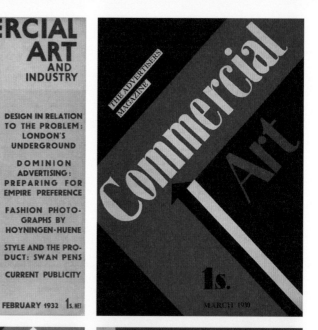

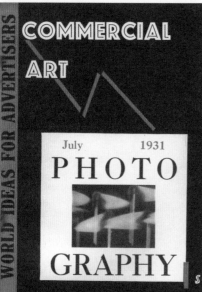

THE 1930s

Besides its usual run of articles on advertising and display the 1930s issues of the magazine reflected such major trends as photography, edging graphics from its central position in press advertisements and posters; typography moving beyond a mere matter of legibility to making an aesthetic contribution; what art schools were actually achieving to introduce design courses, in spite of their bad press; the absorption of the talents of European émigrés into the British design scene; and, most significant of all for the magazine, the arrival of 'Industrial Design'.

Articles on photography had appeared from time to time in the original *Commercial Art*, largely focused on its technical use for reproduction, as it was still novel for use in advertising and publicity. It was not until the 1930s that the magazine must have startled its readers with illustrations of Man Ray's experimental photography, positioning it as a 'fine' art. It is well into the 30s before the magazine announced that a printer, the Baynard Press, was to set up its own photographic studio, using photography not merely as a method of reproduction but for the images it was capable of producing. As was its wont *Commercial Art* was ahead of the field in pronouncing photography not just a technique but an art form, to be taken seriously by the advertising industry. As early as 1931, for its July issue, it carried six articles on the subject, from Saxon Mills writing on 'The Camera Comes into its Own' and Harold Curwen on 'the use of photography in booklets', to features on using colour photography, and devising stunts with photography. Throughout the decade there was hardly an issue that did not carry some aspect of the commercial use of photography.

Although the names of various British photographers would pop up from time to time, including Howard Coster, 'the photographer of the famous', Walter Bird, known for his images of unclothed women, and Norman Parkinson for his women clothed, *Art & Industry*, (as the journal was to be renamed), entrusted many of its later 1930s features to

THE BAYNARD
PHOTOGRAPHIC STUDIO
BLACKWELL STREET, LONDON, S.W.9. TELEPHONE RELIANCE 1211

Advt.

A progressive printer, Baynard Press, with its own photographic studio

a German, Walter Nurnberg (who was also to write for The Studio Ltd *How To Do It* series *The Science and Technique of Advertising Photography*).

Nurnberg had studied at the Reimann School in Berlin, and was to teach there on a part-time basis when it relocated to London. He already had advertising experience before coming to England in 1933. He quickly became fluent in writing in English and was already writing for trade journals when The Studio Ltd called on his services.

Introduced to readers as 'a foremost advertising photographer', Nurnberg wrote a series of articles, from 1935 onwards, under the heading 'A Cameraman's Jottings'. Using both his own work and that of other photographers, he tackled a variety of aspects of advertising photography, as close-ups, or how to make everyday objects eye-catching.

Art & Industry brought him back in again, in the late 1930s, to write a series 'Campaign Camera', to show how the camera could be used to produce different effects that would attract attention, often symbolizing what was being sold rather than simply representing it. One of his examples was his campaign for 'Ostermilk', working with the John Tait advertising agency. For this he didn't resort to showing concerned mothers, but merely had the unclothed back of a baby against a blank background; another, for a Player's cigarette campaign, placed his smokers in ordinary everyday situations, such as in an office. The Campaign Camera series was particularly realistic as it included such aspects of an advertising photographer's work as coping with commissioners, the copy-writers and others – whether the

Nurnberg's original approach for the use of photography in advertising

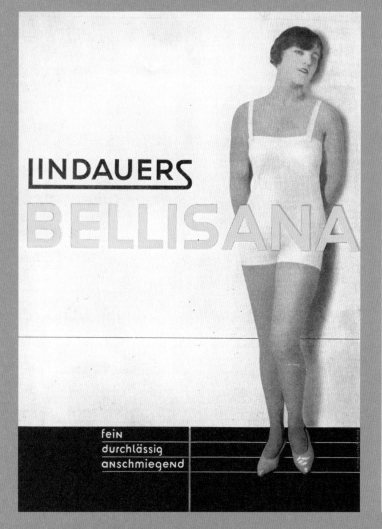

Showcard designed by Jan Tschichold, original printed in silver, 1930

Reproduction of 'Bifur' typeface designed by A.M.Cassandre, 1930

photographer was to work on an already detailed brief, or to be given the freedom to be the visualizer as well. Nurnberg was intent on improving British advertising photography and its professional status and used his articles to this end. By using Nurnberg – a thinking photographer – the magazine was, as with graphics, helping the manufacturer appreciate the contribution that photography could make to his advertising and opening the eyes of young photographers to the opportunities in the advertising field.

As the magazine was to keep the reader updated on photography, it also brought the latest on typography to its pages, more speedily 'with it' than the more earnest and home spun *Penrose Annual*. In the early issues of the magazine typography had been treated in a fairly perfunctory way, perhaps not appreciated as a sufficiently strong weapon in the magazines arsenal for its campaign for building a valid commercial art. Using the word 'lettering', the main issue tackled had been legibility, with the odd attempt to establish criteria as to whether the particular use of lettering for a particular purpose was 'suitable'. This had been specifically written about by the commercial artist Kennedy North, who considered the 'lettering' of the time 'chaotic', and thought that some basic rules might help.

Soon, in the magazine, the word 'typography' began to replace 'lettering', and there was even the nub of an idea of the possibility of such a person as a 'professional typographer' –

'The expert typographer is the man who can clothe good copy in its most suitable and artistic typographical dress.'

There is even an early hint that preference for the ornamental or antique look could give way to something more simple. As with so many of the magazine's writers, on so many aspects of design, such improvements were linked to the 'growth of civilisation! It outed its stand in the July issue of 1930, starting with a nearly blank page with a central text –

'This number presents the first exposition in England of the new conception of typography and the arrangement of the printed page, which has begun already to establish a 20th century style.'

The magazine was announcing the arrival of the ideas of Jan Tschichold on our shores. Tschichold was an early, if not the earliest, typographer to work as a free-lance consultant. Drawing his ideas from what was going on at the Bauhaus, he developed his 'modernist' stance in his *Die Neue Typographie (The New Typography)*, published in 1928. *Commercial Art* followed its preliminary fanfare with some eighteen pages solely dedicated to this new typography, to be followed in subsequent issues by articles by Tschichold himself.

After this initial hullabaloo all fell quiet on the matter of typography until about 1936 when many of the emerging breed of British typographers came to be featured – Francis Meynell, Robert Harling, James Shand, Oliver Simon, and, as it were British by adoption, Beatrice Warde (publicizing what was happening at Monotype). Typography, as a valid profession, was given a sort of royal blessing when, in 1936, the Royal Society of Arts included J.H.Mason, (who had been teaching 'printing' at the Central School of Arts & Crafts), in its first batch of Royal Designers for Industry (RDIs), naming his award as being 'for printing and typography'. There followed a sprouting of typographical journals as Oliver Simon's *Signature* and Robert Harling and James Shand's *Typography* all of this commented upon in *Commercial Art*, now to be titled for a brief spell *Commercial Art & Industry* before settling upon *Art & Industry*. Frederick A. Horn was brought in to write a series of articles on the more popular contemporary types for the advertiser and on the best way to use them; and Robert Harling on the most progressive type foundries, in particular Klingspor and Bauer. This was typography's moment in the limelight, as far as the journal was concerned, for as graphics began to take something of a backseat, it carried typography with it.

What the magazine remained faithful to, throughout, even more so as Europe faced the possibility of war in the late 1930s, was its internationalism. By then it was not only providing its readers with information on role models and competitors from abroad, but was helping establish the émigrés coming to England from the Continent by featuring them. These, coming to London in the 1930s, were to provide the roll call of the next generation of graphic designers and typographers. Some of them only rested for a short while on their way to what they considered might be better opportunities in the States; some came over for specific commissions; whilst many stayed and became naturalised. Jan Tschichold visited on the beck of Lund Humphries in the mid 30s and was given an exhibition,

to return later to revolutionise Penguin's typography in the 1940s, but then return to Switzerland. Jan Lewitt and George Him were also brought across by Lund Humphries but decided to stay. F.H.K.Henrion arrived with a brief from the British Crown Agents but stayed to eventually lead the field for the concept of corporate identity. Others came to London either prescient of what was happening in Germany, or because they became excluded as aliens or Jews, including Berthold Wolpe, Laszlo Moholy-Nagy and Zero (Hans Schleger).

All of these were to be featured in the magazine in one way or another, but possibly some of its strongest émigrés support was given to the persecuted Reimann School, which relocated itself to London in 1936. This school was the most progressive of its kind, offering classes in poster art and advertising even before WWI. The School had already been featured in *Commercial Art* in the 1920s as an example of progressive applied art education, as a role model –

'a school which aims to provide a source of supply for commerce and industry of trained and skilled craftsmen, and to ensure for them the means of making a living.

After the anti-Semitic Nuremburg Laws were passed in 1935, the Reimanns, a Jewish family, did what they could to survive but eventually decided to move the school. In London

Opposite left Booklet cover designed by Lewitt-Him

Opposite right Invitation card designed by Zero (Hans Schleger)

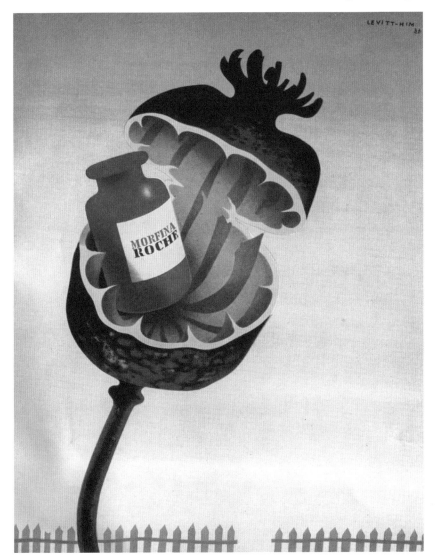

it had four main departments – fashion and dressmaking, display, photography, and later, interior design. With it came as a student Dorrit Dekk (to become known for her travel publicity advertisements), and student turned teacher Natasha Kroll (who was to make her name at Simpson's of Piccadilly and later with BBC Television). Not only did the magazine give generous coverage to the School's arrival, but was, from then on, to show examples of its students' work under such headings as 'Reality in Art School', and to make much of its annual student exhibitions describing them 'a very important force in useful design'; and, a rarity for art schools, that it was able to provide a list of what came to be known as 'first destination statistics' – did courses lead to paid employment – the Reimann list included Cadbury's, Rowntree's, Glaxo and Galeries Lafayette.

Commercial Art, under both ownerships, had previously given little attention to the training of designers as a contribution to the desired relation of art to commerce, so intent was it on furthering that relationship. Where comment did occur it had often been along the lines that British art schools considered commerce grubby. Tom Purvis in a blistering lecture, printed in the magazine in 1937, looking back on his own experiences, implied that even in the 1930s colleges were still 'strangers to commercial practice', still in the age of handicrafts. As late as 1940, *Art & Industry* published a letter from Hal Missingham, an Australian teaching at the Central School of Arts and Crafts –

'The art schools are a pain in the neck both to the manufacturer and the agent. Only incompetents teach

in them, and it is left to the agent or studio to educate the products of the schools into some more lofty pinnacle of initiation when they come looking for work.'

The magazine had previously questioned the purpose of arts schools given that they were publicly funded and

Above Reimann School, Berlin, included Walter Nurnberg as a student
Opposite Salford and Eastbourne Schools of Art prospectuses for feature on art schools 1930s

SALFORD
SCHOOL OF ART

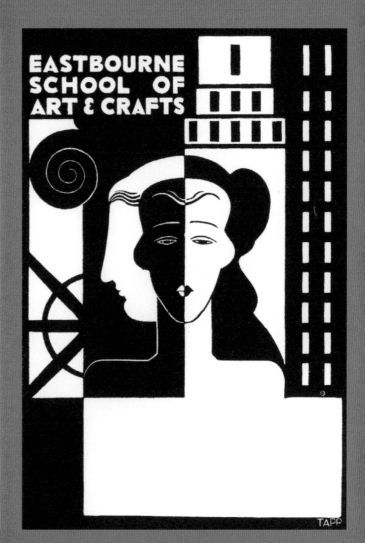

EASTBOURNE
SCHOOL OF
ART & CRAFTS

TAPP

needed to justify their existence. It had not only found art schools wanting, but the government itself indecisive as to whether to use technical colleges or art schools for new design courses, unsure about national certification, and, indeed, without a Chief Inspector to progress things along. Editorials rarely seem to have contributed to the discussion of such matters, and eventually the magazine chose to fall back on merely presenting the most positive work different colleges were producing starting with Brighton, Westminster and Salisbury, and spreading the net wider with two series 'Art Schools that Train for Commerce' and later 'What the Schools are Doing'. All this was imbued with as much of the magazines' perpetual optimism that it could conjure up –

'art schools are awakening to industry's needs.'

At least it could be confident that graphics was, by the mid-1930s, an established course at most art schools, even if other areas of design were lagging behind. What was noticeable was the absence of any mention of The Royal College of Art, a phoenix yet to arise from the ashes.

If photography, typography and émigrés were each to be given its time in the magazine in the 1930s, industrial design not only came to hog the space, but to change the focus of the magazine itself. Although the first issue under The Studio Ltd's proprietorship had been flooded with

Opposite Spread of commercial vehicles including the 'Regent' double-decker bus (bottom right), 1932

good looking products, from Rolls Royce cars and Lalique glass, to Hampton's furniture and even kitchen utensils, its interest in what was going on in manufacturing appears to have died down for a time.

Suddenly, in the 1932 issues, there is a revival, but with excess and sorely in need of editing – nineteen pages on the steel industry, sixteen pages on glass, fifteen on motor vehicles. It is as if the editors knew they should be featuring industrial design matters more, but were themselves unsure of what they were. By 1933 it appears to have got some grasp of the subject and put out another 'announcement', slipping in a little self-congratulations on the way –

'Industrial design is a matter of increasing importance in these days of immense competition; recognized, featured and made use of to the fullest possible extent by our many competitors abroad. And every constructive effort which supplements our own activities in bringing about closer co-operation between art and industry is all to the good and will strengthen our own efforts and the interest taken in them.'

The editors took pride in the fact that their quotation was embodied in the Government's Gorell Report on the encouragement of good industrial design.

In the March 1932 issue it threw down the gauntlet –

'Here is a new adventure for the man of ability and vision.'

'The dean of industrial design' – Walter Dorwin Teague, 1933

– bemoaning the fact that Britain did not appear yet to have such adventurous folk – America was where it was all happening.

'In America are such men as Teague and Norman Bel Geddes – planning today the cars, aeroplanes, and manufactured goods that we shall all be using tomorrow.'

From then on the magazine was to be filled with news and features on the American giants in the field – Walter Dorwin Teague, known as 'the dean of industrial design', and Raymond Loewy, referred to in the press as 'the man who shaped America', leading the pack. Gone are articles on Hungarian packaging and the like, and by the mid-1930s industrial design became the arena for the magazine's missionary message.

From its rather clumsy start there began to flow elegies on all aspects of the subject – as on Loewy's Studebaker and Sears Roebuck refrigerator, on Teague's work with Kodak, on Norman Bel Geddes advocation of 'stream-lining'; in contrast, what was happening in Britain was generally slated. The 'British Art in Industry' exhibition, so feted by those involved, was panned by the magazine as elitist. Teague, who had been asked to comment on a similar exhibition being held at the Metropolitan Museum in New York at about the same time wrote caustically –

'Industrial Design is doing its significant work in quite other fields than dining-rooms and ladies' dressing rooms.'

1930s American stream-lining

Industrial design was to be firmly associated with mass production and with utilitarian products. The only British name that the editors were able to dig up was that of Richard Levin, a name now long forgotten, albeit the product with which he was associated – Bakelite – is now eagerly sought after by collectors. Not just Bakelite, but plastics in general, began to feature in issues towards the end of the decade – from technical details of their production, to examples of 'plastic' products, along with a continuous flow of industrial design news under such headings as 'Design Review' and 'Design Dossier'.

Loewy set up a London office in the mid-1930s and no doubt this stirred the British into action, for tucked away as a news item was the establishment of a design consortium – the Design Unit Ltd., whose Director of Production, Norbert Dutton, was quoted as saying that in Britain –

'...industrial design has not yet been efficiently presented to the manufacturer.'

Dutton was to become a favoured commentator used by the magazine on the subject.

Such was the commitment to furthering the development of industrial design in Britain that both Mercer and Geoffrey Holme, himself, wrote books on the subject in the mid-1930s – *The Industrial Design Consultant* and *Industrial Design in the Future*, respectively. The Design & Industries Association panned Holme's as not arguing the case strongly enough, but merely giving the results of a survey he had done, poorly edited. The critique ended with more than a hint of rivalry when it came to who was contributing more to the growth of industrial design –

> *'The very existence...of such a body as DIA, to which he only refers in the most casual manner, is evidence that it is not such a new thing to adopt his point of view as he suggests.'*

Leaving such competition aside, The Studio Ltd. had definitely begun to shift the focus of the magazine from two to three dimensional design from the beginning of the decade, adding 'and Industry' to its title in 1932, and dropping 'Commercial' in 1936. *Art & Industry* was to remain its title for the next twenty years. The editor wrote of the name change –

> *'The change implies no revolutionary change of policy, but is symbolic of the evolution of the place of the designer in industry.'*

DESIGN WITHOUT DISGUISE

From 1934 to date designers have expressed their ideas for Ekco. I. The Serge Chermayeff model of Season 1933-4 is a bold refusal to disguise, it is frankly radio. 2. A circular cabinet of 1934-5 by Wells Coates. It created a sensation when introduced and still enjoys a vogue. Only by means of plastics could circular cabinets be made. 3. Chermayeff's 1936-7 model shows the versatility of the moulding process. The alternative to figured walnut for this model was black and ivory, a very popular finish. 4. A black and chromium model by Wells Coates. 5. A typical Ekco cabinet by Jesse Collins, 1936-7, featuring large mouldings which are most popular. 6. Season 1937-8 witnesses a knobless cabinet by Ekco Designs Department—spin-wheel tuning and built-in controls. 7. A pick-me-up portable, less than a foot square and weighing 17 lb. by Ekco Designs Department. 8. A television receiver model 1937-8 showing sliding doors closed over screen and controls. 9. Misha Black designed for Season 1937-8 this cabinet which also shows the effect of grain and colour to which plastics lend themselves.

Above Designs for Ekco radios, including designs by Serge Chermayeff, Wells Coates, Jesse Collins and Misha Black

Opposite A timeline spread, 1935

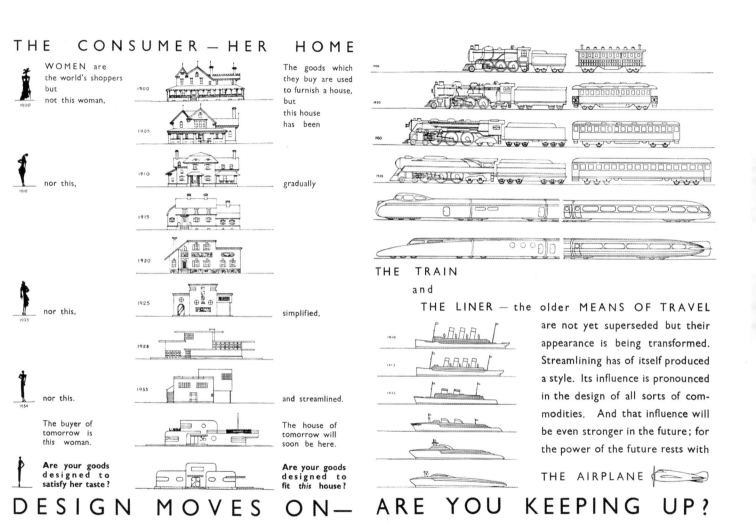

THE CONSUMER — HER HOME

WOMEN are the world's shoppers but not this woman,

nor this,

nor this,

nor this.

The buyer of tomorrow is *this* woman.

Are your goods designed to satisfy her taste?

1900
1905
1910
1915
1920
1925
1928
1933

The goods which they buy are used to furnish a house, but this house has been

gradually

simplified,

and streamlined.

The house of tomorrow will soon be here.

Are your goods designed to fit *this* house?

THE TRAIN
and
THE LINER — the older MEANS OF TRAVEL are not yet superseded but their appearance is being transformed. Streamlining has of itself produced a style. Its influence is pronounced in the design of all sorts of commodities. And that influence will be even stronger in the future; for the power of the future rests with

THE AIRPLANE

DESIGN MOVES ON— ARE YOU KEEPING UP?

Treatment of Bond Street frontage of the Building Centre

designed by Majorie Morrison, 1941

ART & INDUSTRY IN WARTIME

In the issues of the magazine immediately after war had been declared in September 1939, particularly in the December issue, *Art & Industry* looked all set to fight the cause of design and designers when 'production for war was at a flood' and 'styling for commerce at a low ebb'. Employment in Camouflage was hardly going to meet the challenge.

There was a special section set aside titled 'The Artist's Function in Wartime' to which key people were invited to contribute – designers including Milner Gray, Tom Purvis and Betty Prentis, commentators as John Gloag, and administrators, as T.A. Fennimore, the Registrar of the National Register of Industrial Art Designers. They came up with similar comments – that artists actually had skills and approaches that could be of direct use. Gloag in his blustering style –

'But for heaven's sake, lets get out of our heads the idea that the creative designer is a long – haired irresponsible type who is only useful in wartime when he is doing camouflage.'

Betty Prentis and Tom Purvis listed some of the qualities of the designer they felt were relevant – Prentis, of women designers – disciplined, understood business, creative; Purvis – brain, guts, concentration, pioneering, surviving. Milner Gray, by 1939 well used to the benefits of working cooperatively, felt that all organisations concerned with art and design should pool their resources and act as one in utilizing their members' skills. Mentioned were such vague concepts as public morale (make the environment as 'gay' as possible), and culture (remind people what they were fighting for). The more practical suggestions focused on 'exports' – the need to maintain as much overseas trade as possible and to rebuild the economy after the war.

The editors, whilst welcoming such comments, seemed all set, from the beginning, to keep their readers optimistic

and this they continued to do through the ups and downs of the war, much of the magazine devoted to renewal and reconstruction necessary at war end. The December 1939 issue had its editorial titled 'Design for Peace'.

But then, abruptly, in the first issue of the New Year, it was as if the editors were living in a parallel universe – an article on Charles Egri, a Hungarian New Yorker, a feature on American shops, comment on the work of the Carlton Studios, the London Press Exchange's 'before' and 'after' advertising campaign for De Reske cigarettes, and something on art education. The fact that the country had been drawn in to what was to become a world war hardly gets a mention.

Even in the February issue the concern is still with how art and commerce can collaborate, and, a surprise, some references to 'feminine' concerns as Halas & Batchelor's work for Harper's Bazaar. There is one photograph of a shop window boarded up and some Polish war posters, but that's it. And yet again, in the following issue, ten pages on fashion photography and also on Eric Ravilious, Albert Rutherston and Edward Bawden's work for the Kynoch Press, and on the, by then well-established artist, Gregory Brown. And so on, during the Spring, – eight pages on the technique of scraperboard, an article on using stenciling for lettering, another on New York advertising and yet more on fashion photography; in May readers are offered the work of Berthold

....

Opposite Eric Ravilious wood engravings
for a Kynoch Press diary, 1933

Wolpe, thirteen pages on fashion drawing, and a feature on the history of John Grierson's documentary film unit.

Meanwhile Scandinavia is invaded, as is Belgium and the Netherlands. German U-Boats are torpedoing allied shipping, and the Japanese have started their onslaught of China; we retreat from Dunkirk and Churchill delivers his 'we shall never surrender' address.

But in February 1940 paper rationing comes in and the magazine is directly affected. Forced to face up to what was happening beyond Leicester Square, *Art & Industry* shrank, both in page size and in number of pages. The editors can perhaps be forgiven for such previous avoidance behaviour in that the Government, itself, was having difficulty in getting its act together, specifically relevant that part of the Government established to produce wartime information, directives and propaganda – the Ministry of Information. Set up in September 1939 it had little precedence to guide its formation as a similar one started in WWI had been relatively short-lived. The new Ministry became awash with writers, poets, artists, creative souls seeking a safe haven. It took four Ministers and three Director-Generals before, under the efficient hands of Brendon Bracken, it settled to its task –

'..to publicise and interpret Government policy in relation to the war, to help sustain public morale and to stimulate the war effort, and to maintain a steady flow of facts and opinions calculated to further the policy of the Government in the prosecution of the war.'

French Pernod Fils advertisement by Marton, 1940

The World Demands British Goods

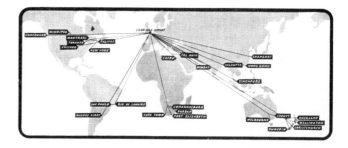
Crawford's patriotic brownie points while self-advertising

It was the Ministry of Information, and some of the more progressive other ministries, that were to provide opportunities for artists and designers during the war – for press announcements, leaflets and booklets, posters and exhibitions. When the wheels started to turn *Art & Industry* had fertile ground to harvest.

Its August issue turned to what was going on in France. The editor not to miss an opportunity to further his cause wrote –

'It is hoped that this French issue, dedicated to those who are fighting on, will provide a reminder of all that France has done – and undoubtedly will do again – in the cause of advertising and its related professions.'

It was not until October that the magazine took up the need to maintain exports, with an export promotion number including contributions from Crawford's Overseas Department, from J. Walter Thompson, and a feature on marketing British cars abroad.

As *Art & Industry* had to face the facts when paper rationing was introduced, it was to be even more intimately acquainted with wartime activity when its Leicester Square premises were fairly totally obliterated in a bombing raid in November. The editor wrote, as cooly as he could, that they had 'suffered great dislocation', and apologized for the late publishing of the magazine!

The bombing of 44 Leicester Square, 1940

'Dashed off' by Tom Purvis, visiting the bomb site.

The company relocated to 66 Chandos Place, just the other side of Charing Cross Road; and there it was to stay for some seventeen years. Repeating, yet again, the magazine's aims of promoting the advantages of good design the Editor bravely wrote –

'Arising from the ashes of its former home, it dedicates itself anew to this service, in the belief that so doing it is making its best contribution to the problems of today.'

By the end of the year, with the Ministries geared up, the December issue was able to have a feature, written by Grace Lovat Fraser, the temporary co-editor, titled 'National Publicity in Wartime'. Soon the magazine had a cornucopia of examples to draw from with the numerous government campaigns – on saving on resources such as metals and food, on staying safe in the blackout, on growing, buying, cooking and eating food economically, on recruitment to the women's services, and so on. With factories pouring out munitions, print rationed, shop windows boarded up, the design of new products non-existent, it was to be the Government who carried so many designers and artists through the war, with employment on information and propaganda assignments.

Through such work designers came to be key players. Milner Gray, whose reputation was in packaging, was appointed in charge of the Government's exhibition programme and quickly built up his own team; Abram Games worked for the War Office on its posters (with his iconic one for WAAF recruitment); F.H.K.Henrion provided posters for the

RAF *War Photos* poster designed by F.H.K.Henrion

Free Europe's Forces poster illustration by Felix Topolski

London Pride poster design by Milner Gray and M.V.Bennett

Ministry of Home Security; Hans Schleger, Lewitt-Him and Eric Fraser posters for the General Post Office; Pat Keely for the Ministry of Labour. Even old-timers were harnessed to the cause, with H.M. Bateman's work on 'coughs and sneezes' for the Ministry of Health, and Frank Newbould, his reputation made in the 1920s, actually working as assistant to Games, a relative new-comer with a thirty year age gap between them.

Besides reporting all this activity the magazine made an all-out effort to include design work from the Dominions, before and after they were drawn into the war, as well as what was going on in allied countries – from America, Russia etc. with a whole issue, in February 1943, devoted to Australian propaganda.

Yet in addition to all this, the magazine could be said to have been contributing to public morale by its perpetually optimistic features on post-war rebuilding. Even as early as when it had been bombed it carried headlines as 'Planning for the Future'. By 1943 it was in full flood –

'The first and most urgent task before us is to win the war, but it is no longer out of order to consider how we shall win the peace that follows it.'

And more fully, and with the usual editorial fervour –

'The new world after the war, as we know, will present gigantic problems and bristle with difficulties, but the volume of them is the measure of opportunities which will

Above 'The violent destruction of war gives an opportunity for rebuilding'
Opposite Comparator table illustrating effectiveness of plastics to boost post-war use (1 is the highest), 1941

PLASTIC MATERIAL	Toughness (Impact Strength)	Flexural Strength	Tensile Strength	Colour	Water Resistance	Acid Resistance	Caustic Resistance	Solvent Resistance	Dimensional Change on Aging	Heat Resistance	Non-Inflamable	Specific Gravity	Hardness
Phenolic: General Purpose	10	3	3	7	6	3	4	1	4	2	3	8	5
Phenolic: Low-Loss	8	3	7	7	3	4	4	1	2	3	1	12	3
Phenolic Heat Resistant	10	4	8	7	3	4	4	1	1	1	1	13	2
Phenolic: Acid and Alkali-Resistant	11	6	8	7	4	2	3	1	5	3	2	5	4
Phenolic: Shock Resistant	2	1	5	7	7	4	5	1	6	3	4	10	5
Phenolic: Transparent	7	1	3	7	4	2	3	1	5	3	2	6	4
Urea	9	1	1	1	9	4	4	1	7	7	5	11	1
Polystyrene	7	4	7	5	1	1	1	3	3	6	6	1	6
Cellulose Acetate	4	6	9	4	11	4	6	3	9	5	6	7	9
Acete-Butyrate	1	5	10	4	8	4	4	3	8	4	6	4	8
Ethyl Cellulose	3	2	6	3	10	4	2	3	8	5	6	2	8
Methyl Methacrylate	6	1	4	2	5	2	2	3	8	9	6	3	7
Vinyl (No Filler)	5	1	2	6	2	1	2	2	3	8	6	9	7

WAR SAVINGS
ARE WARSHIPS

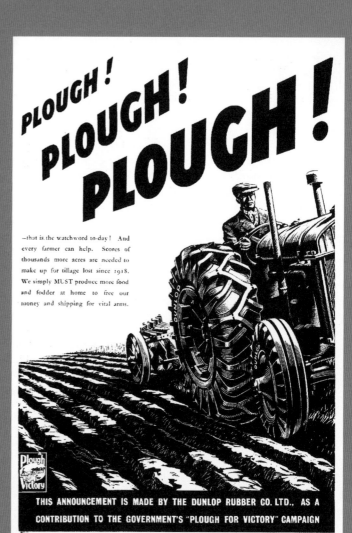

PLOUGH! PLOUGH! PLOUGH!

—that is the watchword to-day! And every farmer can help. Scores of thousands more acres are needed to make up for tillage lost since 1918. We simply MUST produce more food and fodder at home to free our money and shipping for vital arms.

Plough for Victory

THIS ANNOUNCEMENT IS MADE BY THE DUNLOP RUBBER CO. LTD., AS A CONTRIBUTION TO THE GOVERNMENT'S "PLOUGH FOR VICTORY" CAMPAIGN

be presented to those whose faith, vision and enthusiasm, for service spurs them to real endeavour.'

The magazine grasped at any activity, anywhere, that could be used to bolster up morale and to show designers what opportunities lay ahead – a Cotton Board exhibition entitled 'Design for Tomorrow', a review of the RIBA exhibition 'Rebuilding Britain', articles on the future use of prefabrication, the shape of the post-war car, the future use of plastics, and more such.

And, perhaps, without consciously realising it, *Art & Industry* was killing two birds with one stone, when, throughout the war, it included a thin thread on design education – preparing young designers for the future, and encouraging art schools to develop courses relevant to the needs of post-war reconstruction; along with maintaining its campaigning for industrial design, when little of the ilk was actually happening. With little to report from manufacturers, *Art & Industry*, from time to time, during the war years, continued to give factual illustrated accounts of students work in Glasgow and Guilford, in Manchester and Leicester; along with commentaries on related publications as Herbert Read's *Education through Art*, and activities, as those of the Association of Art Institutes. The editorial not only campaigned for more courses on industrial design but for the upgrading of design courses generally, with some to be pitched at a post-graduate level; at one point it even seemed to be arguing for Britain to have a specialist design training institute.

In 1944 the magazine summarized its stance –

'Our art schools have been, with few exceptions, training people in the design of sales propaganda, and, to a lesser extent in the design of handmade products. But the factory will demand more and more industrial designers, men and women who will make the machine the vehicle of their ideas. And to meet this demand we need a new type of School – a school of industrial design.'

Art & Industry can certainly be applauded for keeping its flag flying during the war years – although forced to be small in stature it was large in hope and encouragement. Now it had to face up to the peace it had so enthusiastically and optimistically been writing about; would the reality match up?

Opposite left Government propaganda poster designed by fine artist Norman Wilkinson, R.I.

Opposite right Commercial advertisement by Charles Higham for Dunlop Rubber

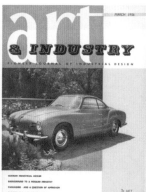

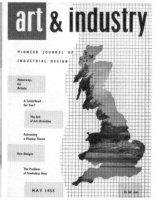

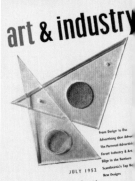

POST-WAR

World War II ended on 2nd September 1945, and *Art & Industry* was now to comment on 'the future' for which it had been encouraging everyone to plan. But that was no easy task for there was little for the magazine to draw upon. Factories were facing the considerable task of having to rejig from munitions to peacetime production, and that would take a considerable time; service personnel returning to jobs needed retraining or at least refreshing; rationing was still in operation until the early 1950s, (paper derationed in 1949); and Europe, the source of so many of the magazines features in the past, needing to reconstruct in every way. *Art & Industry* had to scrape the barrel!

> *'In the hard days ahead initiative and imagination will be tremendous assets helping towards recovery…we can stimulate that.'*

At first the editors delved into the recent past, with such items as how the Dutch had shown such fighting spirit in their wartime propaganda; and from wherever they could,

Above Poster by Nathan for French National campaign for reconstruction

Opposite Post-wartime paper rationing editions, including covers by Zero (Hans Schleger) and Tom Eckersley

from Australia to Finland. Luckily, or possibly not so luckily, was the arrival of the Council of Industrial Design. This had been established at the end of 1944, its objective –

'to promote by all practical means the improvement of design in the products of British industry.'

To demonstrate that it was going to be worth its keep, the Council mounted its first exhibition at the Victoria & Albert Museum in 1946. *Art & Industry* devoted a considerable number of pages to the event, slightly snidely putting forth the opinion that the exhibition showed more the country's skill in exhibition design than in the design of products – so much was being made of so little.

The magazine's early somewhat extravagant enthusiasm for the exhibition –

'"Britain Can Make It" shows that Britain is alive again, ready and able to serve the needs of the world…'

was later to be tempered by seeing it as too selective, neither fairly representing industry nor showing a cross-section of goods the public would buy. In fact it suggested that a conference held during the exhibition was more relevant, and altogether more inclusive, as it involved educationalists, industrialists, exporters, distributors and designers.

Soon everyone was at it, putting on shows and exhibitions, to prove that Britain was making a good recovery. The Export Promotion Department of the Board of Trade restarted the

'Britain Can Make It' exhibition, 1946, furnishing fabric display designed by Jacques Groag

British Industries Fairs held at Olympia and Earls Court, which were also the venue for the Daily Mail Ideal Home Exhibitions and the Society of Motor Manufacturers Motor Shows. And the Council of Industrial Design was back in the fray, joining with the Royal Society of Arts Faculty of Royal Designers for Industry (RDI) to mount the 'Design at Work' exhibition at the Royal Academy. *Art & Industry* refrained from remarking on the subtitle of this exhibition –

> *'an introduction to the industrial designer with a study of his methods of working and the position he holds in British industry.'*

– something the magazine had been doing with crusading fervour throughout the latter part of the 1930s!

However it did make comment when the Council of Industrial Design launched its own magazine *Design* in 1949 (as if through clenched teeth). The Editor wrote –

> *'We may perhaps be forgiven if, as the only journal in the Industrial Design Field for more than twenty years, we preen ourselves a little on our pioneering work and the service we have performed in the national interest. Design is in effect an official endorsement of our effort and pre-vision, for which we are grateful.'*

And the Editor was to continue to stress that Industrial Design was nothing new but that it 'had long been evident', presumably through his journals efforts. By the August

Above left Design Council logo designed by Zero (Hans Schleger)
Above right Opening of the Design Centre, 1956

issue, money talks, and *Art & Industry* was actually carrying advertisements for *Design* on its back pages. By the mid-1950s the magazine seems to have accommodated its challenging bedfellow by reporting, enthusiastically, in 1956, the opening of the Council's Design Centre with its logo designed by Hans Schleger – hyping it as 'the first of its kind in the world'.

All this 'showing off,' with exhibitions and fairs, reached a climax with a national celebration, not so much of 'design' but of being well down the road to recovery – *A Tonic to the Nation* – The Festival of Britain. The magazine started its commentary on this as early as 1949, with an article on Abram Games' symbol for the Festival; and then, once the Festival had started, coverage whilst it ran; and, in 1952, a generous number of pages on the Battersea Festival Gardens, which it considered had generally been disregarded in comparison to what had been going on on the South Bank site. Soon the names of a new generation of exhibition and stand designers began to litter the pages, including Misha Black, James Gardner, Hulme Chadwick and Beverley Pick – Pick commissioned, from time to time, to contribute articles.

Although exhibitions took up a good deal of space in the magazine in the early post-war years, it continued its main push on industrial design. Graphic design was not neglected but certainly took a back seat. Nevertheless there were new relevant series as *Design for Print* – encouraging designers to fully understand the technology for reproducing their work; and Mary Gowing's two series, the first on advertising photographers, followed by *The Creative Mind in Advertising* – praising freelance graphic artists as Hans Schleger and Abram Games and those attached to agencies as Frederick Horn at Booth Waddicor, and Stanhope Shelton at Mather & Crowther. It also continued its features on packaging with Willy de Majo now the occasional expert commentator.

When it came to industrial design, besides articles on specific designers, mainly American, the magazine began a regular feature *New Designs from the Factory*. As early as 1948 *Art & Industry* was stubbornly maintaining –

'industrial design is important, is undiminished and it is steadily and courageously advancing.'

reminding its readers –

'we are still the only British journal specializing in the subject of industrial design.'

Slightly less bullish but perhaps, therefore, more vague, in 1951, it pronounced –

'Until we feel the spirit we shall continue to fail – and feeling the spirit is the essence of good industrial design.'

The magazine, now facing what it considered a lack of progress in British industrial design, began to berate all involved, particularly art colleges offering too limited a range of courses, few actually offering industrial design as such. In 1954, having surveyed what was going on, the editor put his position firmly –

'If the majority of art school products can find no place in industry where their knowledge and training can be of use the fault must lie in the system of training.'

Opposite The Guiness clock designed by Lewitt-Him, Battersea Festival Gardens
Following From a panel by David Gentleman in an exhibition of Irish industrial design, Dublin

How the Industrial Designer works

1 Whether he works on the staff or as an independent consultant, whether he is designing an egg-cup or an aeroplane, the designer tackles his problems in much the same way.

2 First he is briefed by the Management on what is to be designed. He asks many questions, is given all possible details.

5 Now he starts work on the drawing board. He makes many rough sketches, gradually evolving what seems to him the best solution.

6 He has to remember what the machines can do, the limitations of the material, strength, cost, shape, surface, colour, finish.

9 The designer then produces a set of detailed working drawings; sometimes a prototype is made to his specification.

10 After any further modifications, the design goes into production, and the designer checks the first products off the machines to see that they are up to standard.

3 | Then he finds out how the product is made,
what it costs, how it is distributed and sold and who buys it.

4 | He examines competitive products, at home and overseas, talks to retailers
and consumers and finally collates all his research.

7 | With the pick of his sketches, sometimes a 'mock-up', he shows
the Management the result of his preliminary work and explains it.

8 | The designs are discussed and criticized, amended, developed.
Finally there emerges the design which suits all requirements.

11 | Then the new product is packed, distributed, advertised, displayed
and finally sold but by that time the designer is hard at work on
his next problem.

12 | But he takes time off whenever he can to travel, visit exhibitions, read technical
publications, study new materials and processes and so keep always abreast of trends
and fashions.

He made an exception with the Royal College of Art on Robin Darwin's appointment as its Rector and R.D.Russell being made Professor in the School of Furniture and Light Engineering Design.

'The substantial changes in outlook and policy of the Royal College of Art contribute a major event in the evolution of the system of training industrial designers.'

Although claiming no favourites, the magazine seems to have been partial to what was going on at the Leicester School of Art with Kenneth Holme as its Principal, holding that post for some twenty years. At the same time as developing a design course for his students he worked as a consultant designer – from corsets to electricity. Frank Pick who rarely wrote of achievements outside that of his transport empire, wrote of Holme –

'never has anyone been given so much scope and never has anyone done so much for design in industry and a city with so much distinction.'

It would seem that the editor had been justly discerning in his preference, and soon Holme was being commissioned to write for the magazine on designer training, both in this country and in the States.

After chastising the colleges, the magazine turned its wrath on to employers for not giving opportunities to young industrial designers –

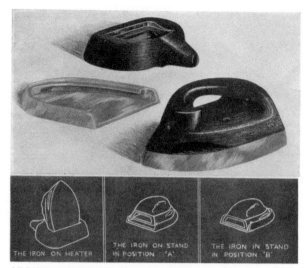

SECOND PRIZE OF £10   DEREK SYDNEY RABLEY
PSEUDONYM "HORNET"

'What may be chicken-feed to a top-line designer of world repute could be bread-and-butter, plus a thick spread of jam, to a lesser known man who has to make a start.'

Art & Industry took a more active role in encouraging the development of industrial design when it started its own industrial design competitions. By getting manufacturers

Above Second prize design in electric iron competition, by Derek Sydney Rabley, 1946

Opposite Misha Black set design (Antelope chairs, 1951, Ernest Race)

involved as sponsors, and students and those working in the field, as competitors, the editor considered he would further general interest in the subject. Firms taking part included Crittall Windows, Yardley and British Industrial Plastics. Launched in 1946, the editor, never backward in his claims, wrote –

Art & Industry competitions are stimulating students and sponsors, are developing keenness and increasing public understanding. Sponsors and entrants are performing a valuable service.'

When the austerity and reconstruction of the immediate post-war years is considered, the magazine had valiantly kept the design flag flying. A new generation of designers was introduced to the reader, from the exhibition designers already listed, to graphic designers including F.H.K.Henrion, Abram Games, and Hans Schleger; for industrial design R.D.Russell, R.Y.Gooden, Misha Black and Gaby Schreiber; and, for textile design, Lucienne Day and Jacqueline Groag – a roll call of the key players in the late 1940s and 1950s.

When *Art & Industry* celebrated its 25th anniversary in 1951, it received congratulations from the great and the good of the design world, beyond the actual designers who had benefitted from being featured. Compliments were given by such worthies as Jack Beddington, formerly of Shell, Ernest Goodale, Chairman of Warner Bros., Fred Philips of the Baynard Press, Sidney Rogerson of I.C.I., Beatrice Warde representing Monotype, Gordon Russell, Director of the Council of Industrial Design, and, from the States, Walter Dorwin Teague – so wide and influential had the magazine's reputation grown. Yet, in spite of all this 'glory', its deathblow was nigh!

Lucienne Day *Graphic* textile design, 1956-57

Jaqueline Groag textiles, 1947

James Gardener exhibition display, 1947

DESIGN

FOR

INDUSTRY

THE HULTON PRESS and
DESIGN FOR INDUSTRY

Design for Industry cover, January 1959

Readers receiving the November issue, in 1957, turning to Mercer's editorial, usually on design about to save civilisation, would have been startled by its content. Not only did Mercer announce a change of address – from Chandos Place to Fleet Street, but a change of ownership; The Studio Ltd. now had a new proprietor – The Hulton Press. Geoffrey Holme, who had steered the ship through calm and stormy waters, had transferred ownership to his sons, Rathbone and Bryan, in the early fifties, but had died, untimely, in 1954, too soon after for the company to avoid heavy death duties, to cover which shares needed to be sold.

It is clear why The Studio Ltd. might have been forced to sell; what is more problematic, is why the Hulton Press chose to buy. Edward Hulton, himself, was not without interest in graphic design. In an article he had written for the *Penrose Annual* on *Picture Post* he had shown as much competence in writing about its presentation as its content; and he had contributed to the Advertising Creative Circle's experimental

ACC Hulton Scholarships. Yet at the time mayhem reigned in Fleet Street, with rival factions buying and selling and merging and rebranding. Why would a Press that was having to shut-down one of its most popular magazines – *Picture Post* – consider it advantageous to buy a specialist design journal. It was a tumultuous time for Fleet Street and a particularly rocky time for the Hulton Press.

Mercer reassured his readers that the thirty year old *Art & Industry* was not contemplating any radical changes and, ever optimistic, and, by now getting rather avuncular in tone, wrote –

'We of the past era will continue with the new and we look forward with confidence and enthusiasm to a time of expansion, advancement and new endeavour.'

And, indeed, through to the Autumn nothing did seem to change, either in the format or the content of the magazine. Series, including 'The Art of Packaging' and Mary Gowing's 'The Creative Mind in Advertising' continued; and new series were started such as 'Campaigns with Courage' and 'Product Promotion Techniques'; overseas news featured in most issues, mainly from America, but also from Europe, Japan and even East Germany; along with news on new products, demonstrating that it was still up to the minute with a feature on Comet IV versus Boeing 707.

But, come November, Rathbone Holme's name no longer appears as Editor, and although Mercer's is still there as Consultant Editor, Wilfred Walter [who he?] suddenly appears as Editor. And in the December issue the bombshell comes – the title *Art & Industry* is to go, to be replaced by *Design for Industry*. There is not only to be a change of title but a change of size – bigger dimensions, more pages. The new Editor explains the shift is because of the increasing importance of industrial design –

'We feel Art & Industry should be more up-to-date. It should widen its scope to bring you, the reader, reliable information and independent comment on all facets of industrial design together with a more comprehensive service of illustration.'

This must not only have affronted Mercer, but have puzzled subscribers, as this is what the magazine had been doing for years. The new Editor finishes with rather vaguely expressed intentions of the January issue 'showing people using products', and that it would be 'a human document'. The loyal reader could well wonder at what was to come!

Come January 1959 *Design for Industry* arrives, sub-titled *Independent International Journal of Industrial Design*, and, in small type 'incorporating *Art & Industry* and *Commercial Art*'. Its Editor is declared as Wilfred Walter, with Mercer still there hovering in the background, named as Consultant Editor. But he now has a co-consultant, Hugh Sutherland (the M.A. after his name giving a flavour of academia). And

Opposite 'Artistic' use of colour for effect rather than legibility

Non-corrodible nuts and bolts produced from block Cobex

Hugh Sutherland on Transport

Armstrong Siddeley Star Sapphire

Cunarder, Queen Elizabeth

Trans-Europe Express of German Federal Railways

The Dayton Albatross

there is another new name added to the credits, Anthony Adams – for the first time the journal names an Art Editor.

And 'arty' it is, from the start. Not only have the dimensions increased, but the cover to the January issue is clearly 'designed' – with four horizontal elongated triangles, overlaid with photography. The reader would instantly be aware that *Design for Industry* would be strikingly presented within – wide margins, self-conscious lay-outs, strong titling – and with supposedly attractive splashes of colour, pink, yellow and pale blue, actually reducing legibility, particularly when overlaying illustrations.

And along with all this novelty came a new generation of writers – commentators on design. Adolf Morath on photography (himself a specialist in industrial photography); Hugh Sutherland (whose name was soon to be removed from co-consultancy) was to be the expert of all things that travelled – from the latest aircraft and helicopters to mopeds, and, of course, the magazine's long term favourite – trains. And there was to be two female writers – Marie-Jacqueline Lancaster (a hardened fashion journalist, design editor of *The Ambassador*), who, nevertheless, seems to have felt equally confident in commenting on bathroom basins and door knobs; and Mary Gilbert, from the British Electrical Development Association, who was well experienced to comment on electrical products, from home power to toasters. Neither of these had a background in advertising, as had Mary Gowing, showing the magazine's entire shift of focus.

But, when it came to writing, the real novelty was to be a regular feature from Maurice Rickards, entitled *It Occurs to Me*. Rickards, a graduate of the Royal College of Art and later the founder of the Ephemera Society, had worked as a free-lance designer, particularly for 'good causes'. His articles for *Design for Industry*, perhaps falling short of being described as 'literary', were nevertheless clever, witty and sharp, a style new to The Studio Ltd. Typical was a piece, supposedly on packaging, but worth quoting for it illustrates the shift in tone that had come with the Hulton ownership –

'As part of its intensive new hydro-nuclear, omni-circuit Widget Development Plan, a Peruvian firm (lets say) need a quarter of a million double-acting megodes (lets say). So inquiries go out to several of the world's leading megode manufacturers. Replies are as follows: British; a letter (in English) to the effect that if the Peruvians care to come over and go into the matter, there may be some chance of doing business; but it is pointed out that delivery time would in any case be 18 months.'

A further shift in the magazine's focus was a kowtowing to business magnates, who were featured individually, rather as individual designers had previously been done in *Commercial Art* and *Art & Industry*. There is an odd nod to the likes of Milner Gray and Walter Teague, but altogether more space was devoted to potential commissioners of design. The roll call was impressive, including Colin Anderson of the Orient Line, Miles Thomas of Monsanto Ltd, Whitney Straight of Rolls Royce, Cecil Weir of ICT, Lord Chandos of AEI and Arthur Gordon Norman of The House of de

Business Sponsors of Design

Whitney Straight, Rolls Royce

Cecil War, ICT

Colin Anderson, Orient Line

Sir Miles Thomas, Monsanto Ltd.

La Rue. *Design for Industry* continued to report on the latest designed products – scooters, television, computers, the Comet, and such, but the shift was definitely towards where the money lay.

Internationalism continued but in a new way, that of having précis of the issue's articles, initially in French, but then in German and Italian as well, on green paper, standing clear from the rest of the journal.

The word 'sophistication' perhaps best describes the repackaging of the journal. It came to look more like a glossy magazine, its writing was sharper and wittier, and it was addressing itself more to company boards than art directors or advertising agents.

But such a gamble, in such economic circumstances, was to prove costly. The December 1959 issue had a nearly all white front page with the copy placed in the centre in large type –

'End of Line'
'The Directors of Studio Ltd, Hulton Press, have reluctantly decided that this, the December issue for Design for Industry, will be the last.'

The reasons given – rise in costs, a reluctance to lower quality standards, and its rather niche market. In spite of its obvious commercial failure, the magazine, as always, did not resist a little self-congratulation, even at its end –

'We believe that Design for Industry during the past year, has added an important chapter to the integrative literature of design and has, perhaps, given impetus to future progress by indicating the true practical function of design as a potent factor in competitive marketing.'

END OF THE LINE

The Directors of Studio Limited, Hulton Press, have reluctantly decided that this, the December issue of **Design for Industry**, will be the last. Their decision follows the recent increase in costs which has made the production of this journal economically impossible without the severe reduction of its present quality, and such reduction would be contrary to our editorial policy.

The remaining Studio publications—Studio magazine and the annuals, *Modern Publicity* and *Decorative Art*—have a wider market than **Design for Industry**, and are consequently in no way affected by the decision.

Design for Industry was first published in January 1959, replacing *Art and Industry* which had covered the field of industrial design for many years. It was, in fact, the first journal in Britain to recognise the designer's growing influence in industry and did valuable service in helping to establish the position he holds today.

We believe that **Design for Industry** during the past year, has added an important chapter to the interpretive literature of design and has, perhaps, given impetus to future progress by indicating the true practical function of design as a potent factor in competitive marketing. In closing we thank all those who have supported our venture.

Mid 1950s Design Journals

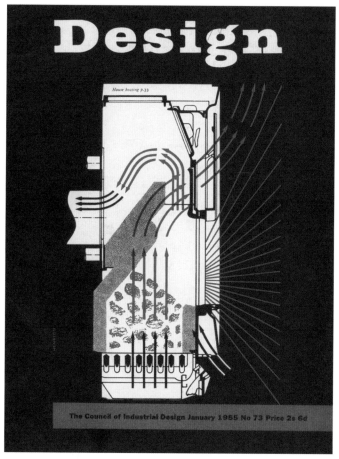

Monthly publications *Art & Industry* published by The Studio Ltd.

and *Design* published by Council of Industrial Design

EPILOGUE

Commercial Art /Art & Industry claimed that during its lifetime it was the only industrial design magazine in Britain until the Council of Industrial Design brought out *Design* in 1949.

In this it was largely correct. The Design & Industry Association's *Design for Today* and the Bernard Jones Publications *Industrial Art, the magazine of applied art in manufacturing and marketing*, both published in the 1930s, although admirable, were relatively short-lived affairs. Furniture and furnishings design was left largely to The Studio Ltd.'s *Decorative Arts Yearbook*; and fashion largely to women's magazines apart from a few instances where there had been striking advertising, as with Austin Reed.

Although there is neither statistical nor Mass Observation-type anecdotal evidence to validate the journal's influence, there seems little doubt of its contribution to the building of 'design' as a profession, by its continually exploring the skills and knowledge required for such professionalism and by the repositioning of the designer's role in any project. The magazine helped to shift 'design' from mere ornamentation at the end of production, to a more integrated role at its start; albeit falling a shade short of the courage needed to suggest that a designer could actually act as a change agent. As it initially had been the leading crusader for graphic design, it certainly pioneered the cause of design for industry.

By featuring designers individually, (whether emerging from art school or, as émigrés, trying to establish themselves in a new country), the magazine gave many the kind of exposure needed for their career development, for students, often the first publicity they would have received. Its features

Annual publications *Modern Publicity* published by The Studio Ltd.

and *Penrose Annual* published by Lund Humphries

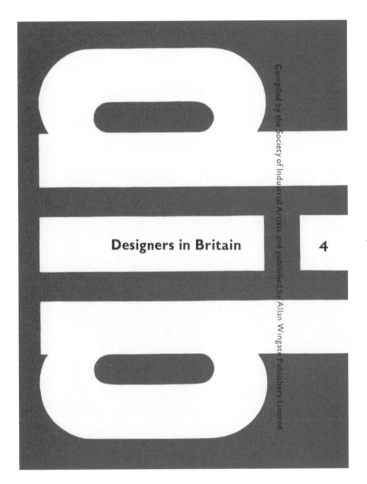

Occasional publication *Designers in Britain* published by
Society of Industrial Artists

on design education and on specific art colleges would well have stirred the slumbering and complacent into action, and, for some, this could well have been a matter of survival as a separate institute.

The internationalism that The Studio Ltd brought to the reader, challenging British parochialism and insularity, must have helped the designer and the commissioner, both by demonstrating the competition, and by providing role models for personal and organisational development. This was particularly the case with industrial design, where the Americans were so far ahead.

The magazine's success and longevity can largely be attributed to three generations of one family – the Holmes – Charles, his son Geoffrey, and, in turn, his sons Bryan and Rathbone – and to one editor-cum-business manager – Frank Alfred Mercer. It became essential reading for designers and their commissioners at the time, and, remains, still, a major source of information for those interested in the history of British design in the first half of the 20th century.

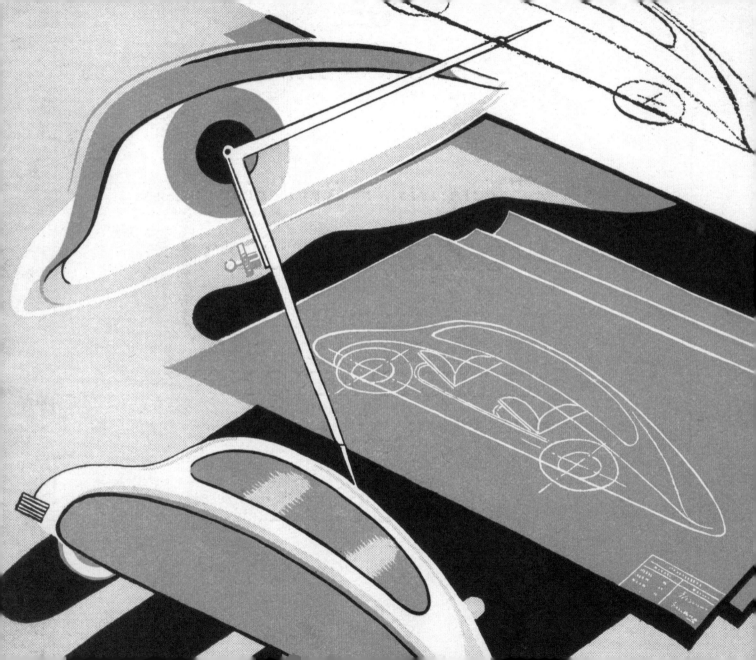

APPENDIX I

Design 'Events' In Britain 1922–1959

1924–5	*British Empire Exhibition,* Wembley
1926	Empire Marketing Board Publicity Committee
1930	Founding of Society of Industrial Artists
1932	Gorrell Report on the production and exhibition of articles of good design and everyday use.
1934	Founding of Basset-Gray Group
1935	*British Art in Industry* Exhibition, Royal Academy
Mid 1930s	Founding of Design Unit Ltd.
	Raymond Loewy establishes London office
1936	Royal Society of Art Royal Designer for Industry (RDI) awards started
1937	Pevsner's *An Inquiry into Industrial Art in England* published
1937	Reimann School opens in London
1939	Ministry of Information in action
1943	Design Research Unit founded
1944	Council of Industrial Design (CoID)
1946	*Britain Can Make It* exhibition V&A
1948	Robin Darwin appointed Rector Royal College of Art
1948	*Design at Work* exhibition Royal Academy
1949	CoID launch *Design* magazine
1951	Festival of Britain
1956	Design Centre opened
1959	Misha Black- Professor of Industrial Design RCA

Opposite Art & Industry 1943 cover designed by Paul B.Mann

APPENDIX 2

Some 'people' series from the magazine

A. Published from 1923 onwards *Artists who helped the Advertiser*

Graham Simmonds	Aubrey Hammond
Fred Taylor	Tom Purvis
Charles Pears	Alfred Taylor
Arthur Ferrier	Edmund J.Sullivan
Christopher Clark	Austin Cooper
Rilette	The Dorian Workshop
McKnight Kauffer	Frank Newbould
Gregory Brown	Eric Fraser
Aldo Cosomati	Nora Schleger
Horace Taylor	H.M.Bateman
Dillon McCurk	Fred Pegram
Foster	Harold Nelson
The Zinkheisen sisters	Septimus Scott

B. Published from 1928 onwards, drawn by 'bil', Henry Ospovat, and Aubrey Hammond – *Celebrities of Advertising, Personalities in Publicity*

Mr.H.Gordon Selfridge	Mr.Fred Taylor R.I.'
Mr.Frank Pick	Sir Charles F.Higham
Sir William S.Crawford	Rt.Hon.C.A.McCurdy K.C.
Mr.C.G.G.Dandridge	Mr.C.Harold Vernon

C. Published from 1952 onwards *Advertising that Advertises*

Colman, Prentis, Varley	Greenley's
Cecil B.Notley	Booth Waddicor
W.S.Crawford	London Press Exchange
Charles H.Higham	C.R.Casson Ltd.
Pritchard, Wood & Partners.	N.W.Ayer [N.Y.]
Stuart's	

D. Published from 1956 onwards *The Creative Mind in Advertising* written by Mary Gowing

Hans Schleger	Frederick A.Horn
Ashley	Eric Hobbs
Stanhope Shelton	Ruth Gill
Arpad Elfer	Phillip Boydell
Harry Ballam	Tom Eckersley
George Him	Jack Beddington
Abram Games	Mary Gowing [by Ballam]

E. Published from January 1959 in *Design for Industry* – *Profile of an industrialist*

Sir Colin Anderson	Sir Miles Thomas
Whitney Straight	Lord Chandos
Sir Cecil Weir	

ACKNOWLEDGEMENTS

My gratitude goes to Chris Mees the generous book dealer who introduced me to *Commercial Art* some decades ago; to my designers, Brian Webb and Abi Hood of Webb & Webb for their enthusiasm and creative solutions; and not least, to Eduardo Sant'Anna for his help in arduous task of getting the illustrations together.

The February 1925 cover by Royal Academician Hendy
(William M. Hendy) who drew humorous illustrations for *Punch*
and Fortnum & Mason translates art into commerce

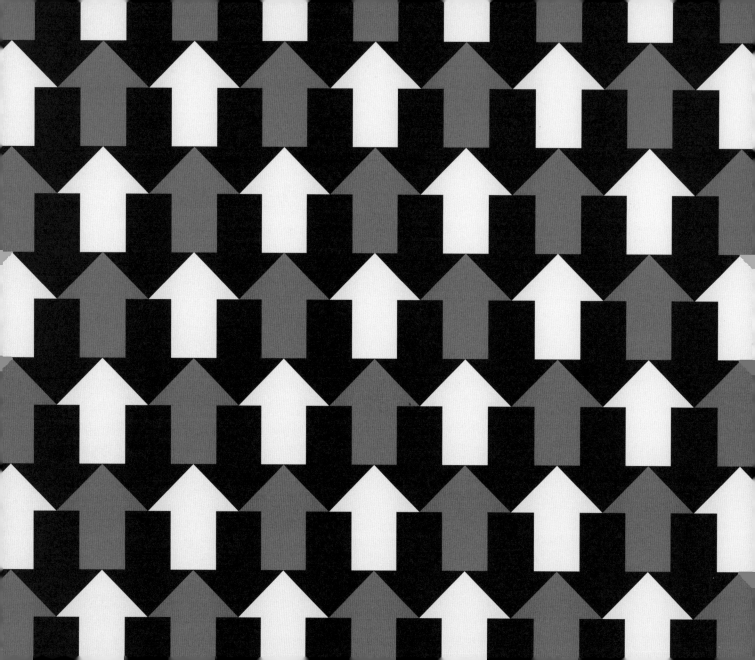